The Progressive Movement 1900–1920
Efforts to Reform America's New Industrial Society ™

PROSECUTING TRUSTS

The Courts Break Up Monopolies in America

Bernadette Brexel

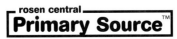
rosen central
Primary Source ™

The Rosen Publishing Group, Inc., New York

Published in 2006 by The Rosen Publishing Group, Inc.
29 East 21st Street, New York, NY 10010

First Edition

343.73
Brexel

Library of Congress Cataloging-in-Publication Data

Brexel, Bernadette.
Prosecuting trusts: the courts break up monopolies in America / by Bernadette Brexel.
    p. cm. — (The progressive movement 1900–1920: efforts to reform America's new industrial society)
Includes bibliographical references and index.
Contents: Big business and trusts—The public and progress—Bringing big business under control—Setting up business rules for good—The legacy of prosecuting trusts.
ISBN 1-4042-0188-2 (lib. bdg.)
ISBN 1-4042-0857-7 (pbk. bdg.)
6-pack ISBN 1-4042-6193-1
1. Antitrust law—United States—History—Juvenile literature. 2. Progressivism (United States politics)—Juvenile literature. [1. Antitrust law. 2. Progressivism (United States politics)]
I. Title. II. Series.
KF1649.6.B74 2004
343.73'0721–dc22

2003022033

Manufactured in the United States of America

On the cover: Top: A photograph of the justices of the U.S. Supreme Court, circa 1894. Bottom: A photograph of the Standard Oil Company, Richmond, California, circa 1913.

Photo credits: Cover (top), p. 18 photograph by C. M. Bell, Collection of the Supreme Court of the United States; cover (bottom) courtesy of Library of Congress Prints and Photographs Division; p. 5 (left) Robert N. Dennis Collection of Stereoscopic Views, Miriam and Ira D. Wallach Division of Art, Prints, and Photographs, The New York Public Library, Astor, Lenox, and Tilden Foundations; p. 5 (right) Rare Book, Manuscript, and Special Collections Library, Duke University; p. 6 © Museum of History & Industry/Corbis; p. 7 © AP/Wide World Photos; p. 8 Brown Brothers; p. 10 American Social History Project, New York; pp. 12, 21 (inset) © Corbis; p. 15 Map Division, The New York Public Library, Astor, Lenox, and Tilden Foundations; p. 16 © North Wind Picture Archives; p. 20 Old Military and Civil Records, National Archives; p. 21 © Bettmann/Corbis; p. 22 The Rod Kennedy Postcard Collection; p. 26 © Hulton Archive/Getty Images.

Designer: Les Kanturek; Editor: Mark Beyer; Photo Researcher Amy Feinberg

Contents

Chapter One

Big Business and Trusts

Businesses sell goods or services. Goods are things such as clothing and furniture. A service is something you use. Electricity is a service. A business does well if the public buys its goods and services.

It is very good when a business does well. The business will grow. It brings money into a town or city. More jobs open up for the public. A growing business uses the goods and services of other businesses. These businesses will grow, too.

Other businesses may decide to sell the same goods or services. Another business that sells the same goods or services is a competitor. Competitors compete for the same customers.

When two competitors do well, it is also very good. Each competitor tries to make the best goods or services. Competitors will invent new things. The quality of the

Small businesses, such as this store in New York, could barely compete against large businesses for customers. When large businesses bought more goods at a cheaper rate, they could charge less money than the small businesses. They advertised *(upper right)* cheaper rates for goods. Hundreds of small businesses closed in the late 1800s because of the way big business set their prices.

goods or services gets better. One competitor may drop prices to get more customers. Another competitor may drop prices to compete. The public will pay less for better goods and services.

Competitors try to make things easier and faster. They try to make things for very little money. Businesses that

5

cannot do the same will close. New businesses will then try to compete. Everyone gets a chance at success. This is because competition is not limited.

America was growing in the middle and late 1800s. This was a good time for business. Many people moved to America from other countries. The growing public needed

Railroads brought goods to people in towns and cities from distant factories. This sawmill made lumber that helped build the growing cities across America. The train companies charged unfair rates to carry the lumber, however. They could do this because mills had no other choice for transportation of their goods.

many goods and services. Goods included lumber, coal, steel, oil, food, and clothing. Services included mail and gas. Goods not found in America were shipped from overseas. A company with hard-to-find goods could quickly make a fortune.

Many businesses, big and small, enjoyed great success. Things changed around the 1860s. Wealthy owners such as John D. Rockefeller changed how business was done. The owners wanted to stamp out all competitors. Then the owners could be in charge of everything. By controlling the making, selling, and buying of goods and services, they could control the market.

John D. Rockefeller made Standard Oil into one of the largest monopolies in America. The Progressives fought to have the federal government break up the company for its bad business practices.

There are many ways to stamp out a competitor. One way is to buy the competitor's business. The competitor becomes a part of the larger business. This is called a merger.

Some mergers do not have happy endings. A business can buy a smaller company and close it. Then, hundreds of people lose their jobs. Customers of the small company

VOL. XXV.—No. 630.   NEW YORK, MAY 1, 1889.   PRICE, TEN CENTS.

KEPPLER & SCHWARZMANN, Publishers.

WHO IS IN THE SOUP NOW?

Political cartoons helped to tell the public about the hardships of small businesses and working people. Here, the working man is drowning in government legislation aimed to help big business.

are forced to buy from the larger company.

Another way to control competitors is to create a trust. A trust is a deal between big businesses. Big businesses join together to control the making, selling, and buying of goods or services. A trust controls the market for those goods or services. This is also called a monopoly.

Trusts stop smaller businesses from getting the things they need. These things include materials, store owners, and customers. They charge high prices so that the smaller businesses cannot afford the materials.

The trust makes sure that fewer goods or services are offered to the public. It then raises the prices of goods or services. Because there are fewer goods, the public has to pay the high prices.

Chapter Two

The Public and Progress

L ife gets better when businesses compete. Goods and services are better. New ways of doing things are invented. The public can choose from many different goods and services. Prices are low, so the public saves money. With more money, the public can buy more needed things. This is called progress.

Trusts worked against progress. While trusts grew bigger and wealthier, the public suffered. The public had to pay high prices. People did not get a choice of goods and services. They had to buy whatever the trusts made and sold. Trusts limit competition.

Trusts also worked against workers. Workers were told to work very hard. If a worker did not work hard enough, he or she was replaced. Some trusts made their own factories compete against each other. If one factory failed, the trust closed the factory. Trusts tried to get things made without

Working people began to fight back against big business. A steelworkers' union strike in Homestead, Pennsylvania, turned deadly in 1892. Owner Andrew Carnegie ordered armed guards to help strikebreakers get into the factory. Armed steelworkers fought the guards. The union was broken, and many men died during the protests.

paying their workers enough money. Workers had horrible lives. They had little money to show for all their work. They could not even afford healthy, safe housing.

During the 1870s, the public began asking for better lives. People wanted progress. Eventually, these people became known as Progressives. They started the Progressive movement. The movement was most active from 1900 to 1920. This is known as the Progressive Era.

Progressives wanted better lives. They wanted better and safer workplaces. They wanted fair prices for goods and services. They also wanted big business to stop forming trusts. Journalists wrote important stories to reach the public. Many stories told of unfair business practices.

Progressives wanted to change the government. They wanted leaders who would fight against trusts. Many leaders

U.S. Steel Corporation

In 1898, Congress created the Industrial Commission. The commission watched for trusts. It filed reports on trusts. From 1887 to 1897, more than eighty-six trusts were formed. Between 1898 and 1900, 149 more trusts formed. Trusts controlled railroads, steel, oil, and sugar. The United States Steel Corporation was one of the largest trusts. It included eleven major companies. It controlled more than 85 percent of the iron ore in the United States.

The trust forced many small steel companies out of business. One report stated that workers worked seven days per week. They worked twelve-hour days. They were paid very little. More than 65 percent of the workers could not afford to keep their families safe or healthy.

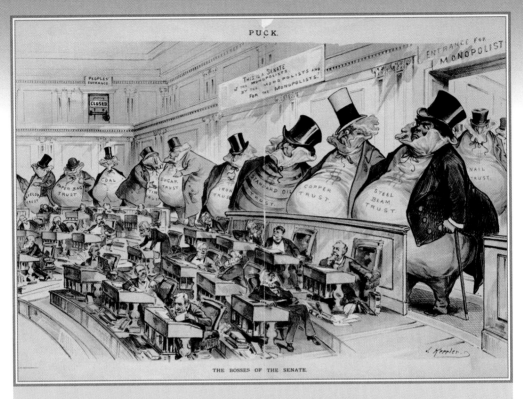

U.S. senators were accused of helping the big-business trusts keep their powerful hold on the economy. In this political cartoon, the fat trust owners sit behind the small legislators working at their desks. The names of the trusts are written on the owners' bellies.

were friends with wealthy business owners. They were not against trusts. The Progressive leaders slowly moved into government jobs in order to help change laws.

The first major law against trusts was passed in 1890. It was the Sherman Antitrust Act. It was also known as the

Antitrust Act. The law made it illegal for big companies and trusts to limit competition. "Illegal" means against the law. The Antitrust Act was not perfect, though. The way it was written was not clear. Officials could not agree upon what the law meant. Some believed the law was against all trusts. Others believed the law was only against trusts selling goods and services within each state.

Chapter Three

Bringing Big Business Under Control

At first, little was done to use the Antitrust Act. The first antitrust case went to the Supreme Court in 1895. It was called *United States v. E. C. Knight Company*. The trust was the American Sugar Refining Company.

The trust controlled more than 80 percent of the U.S. sugar business. Competitors said the trust wanted to control prices. The case was dropped. This meant that the sugar trust was not stopped. Wealthy business leaders were happy about the case. It meant that they could keep forming trusts.

A successful case against trusts was won in 1897. It was called *United States v. Trans-Missouri Freight Association*. The trust was made of eighteen different companies. The trust wanted to fix prices for railroad service. Businesses west of the Missouri River accepted the new prices. A Kansas court dropped the case. The judge decided the

Railroad trusts worked to fix prices across all their transport lines. This meant that most of America had to pay the same price for getting their goods to market. This hurt small businesses' ability to compete. The Supreme Court took its first steps toward stopping railroad trusts in 1897.

Antitrust Act did not include laws about price-fixing. The case went before the Supreme Court. The Court decided against the trust. It ordered the trust to break apart.

In 1901, Theodore Roosevelt became president. He was not against big business. He was against trusts that limited competition. He became known as the "trust buster." He started the Bureau of Corporations in 1903. It

Theodore Roosevelt took charge of busting up trusts when he became president of the United States in 1901. He opened up investigations into trusts and their connection to the government. He also used the government to take trusts to court for unfair business practices.

was a government group that watched businesses. If a business broke the law, the government sued it. The business was brought before a court to answer the charges. More than forty companies were sued during Roosevelt's presidency. There were trusts in the tobacco, meatpacking, salt, paper, coal, and furniture industries.

Another important case was *Northern Securities Company v. United States*. It began in 1902. Wealthy railroad owners tried to buy the stock of other railroad companies. Stocks are shares of a company. With enough shares, a person can control that company. This would give Northern Securities control of the railroad lines. The lines reached from the Pacific Ocean to the Great Lakes.

The Supreme Court decided against Northern Securities in 1904. It stopped the company from controlling other rail companies.

First Trust Breakup

The Standard Oil Company started the very first trust in 1879. John D. Rockefeller owned the company. He bought out many of his competitors. More than forty companies became part of the Standard Oil Trust. It controlled more than 90 percent of the oil production and distribution in the United States.

The Standard Oil Company was taken to court in 1906. By then there were more than seventy companies involved. Charges against the trust included:

- Controlling pipelines
- Limiting competitor business
- Price-fixing

The court decided against the trust in 1909. The Supreme Court agreed in 1911. It broke the trust into different competing companies. Some later became Exxon, Mobil, and Amoco.

By 1904, the Supreme Court had broken up many trusts. But trusts were still formed. Some judges on the Court did not see all trusts as bad. Others wanted to break up each trust that was formed. The Sherman Antitrust Act did not force the end of trusts for many years.

Trusts kept forming. It was hard to make trusts follow the law. Court judges made opposite decisions over the Antitrust Act. Some judges saw trusts as bad and illegal. Other judges approved of trusts.

William Taft became president in 1909. He wanted more control of trusts. Seventy-eight companies were brought up on trust charges. Most of the cases did not get to court until the next president. Woodrow Wilson became president in 1912. Wilson wanted stronger antitrust laws, too.

Chapter Four

Setting Up Business Rules for Good

T wo very important acts were passed in 1914. Congress passed the Federal Trade Commission Act. It also passed the Clayton Antitrust Act.

The Federal Trade Commission Act set up the Federal Trade Commission (FTC). The FTC makes sure that antitrust laws are followed. The commission has many powers. It can investigate businesses. It can request company reports and publish its findings. The FTC files a complaint if it finds a business breaking the laws. The business has a chance to prove its innocence. If the FTC finds the business guilty, it can issue an order. The order tells the business to stop unfair business practices. If the business does not stop, the FTC takes the business to court. The FTC also meets with industry leaders. The industry leaders talk about fair and unfair business practices.

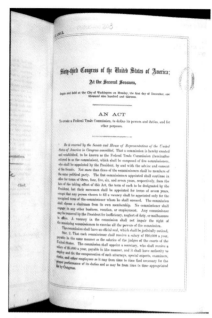

Newer laws were needed to help the Sherman Antitrust Act. The Federal Trade Commission was formed in 1914. The commission worked to pass laws that made trusts and monopolies illegal. It also worked to bring businesses to court for cheating consumers and competitors.

The Clayton Antitrust Act was made to support the Sherman Antitrust Act. It stopped businesses from creating monopolies. Businesses could not fix prices for one customer and not another. Price-fixing was not allowed if it would limit competition.

The Clayton Act stopped businesses from trying to limit competition. Any monopoly that formed to limit competition was illegal. Mergers were illegal if they would limit competition. Businesses were also banned from buying each other's stocks.

Business leaders were tricky, though. They began to buy the assets of a competitor instead of stocks. Assets are company resources such as real estate or property. A merger could still happen by buying up a competitor's assets.

The New York Stock Exchange (above) was a place for businesses to sell shares in their companies to raise money. Sometimes big businesses bought shares in smaller businesses to take over those companies. One example was Swift & Company, which bought enough shares in other meatpacking companies (inset) that it took over the entire meatpacking market.

An important decision happened in 1932. The case was *United States v. Swift & Company*. The case started in 1920. Swift & Company formed a monopoly in the meatpacking market. The company began to buy stocks and companies in other markets. It was involved with

The United States sued Paramount Pictures because of its monopolistic practices in the filmmaking industry. Paramount had violated the Clayton Antitrust Act by limiting competition. The United States went after the largest companies because their size alone proved that they were using monopolistic practices to beat their competitors.

dairy and newspapers. It was attempting to form monopolies in these markets, too.

The company had broken the Clayton Act laws. It limited competition by its actions. The judge also decided that the size of the trust was enough to prove that it was a monopoly. This decision meant that it would be easier to go after big business groups. If a business group was too large, it could be considered a monopoly. The same decision was reached in *United States v. Paramount Pictures*.

In 1936, the Robinson-Patman Act was passed. It supported the Clayton Act.

Illegal Trust Activities

- Monopolies that limit competition and free trade
- Price-fixing too low to drive out competitors
- Price fixing between competitors to control a market
- Agreeing with competitors to limit goods and services
- Giving discounts only to special customers, clients, buyers, and manufacturers
- Purchasing a competitor's stock or assets

It made all price-fixing illegal. No business or group of businesses was allowed to give discounts to favorite customers. The Celler-Kefauver Act was passed in 1950. It made buying another business's assets illegal. A merger was illegal if it would limit competition.

Chapter Five

The Legacy of Prosecuting Trusts

Strong antitrust laws are good. The government can watch big business. Hundreds of antitrust cases have been filed. Cases have included trusts for interesting goods and services. These include blackboards, buttons, candy, eggs, flowers, rabbit skins, taxicabs, and umbrellas. Wherever there was a business, there was a chance for a trust or monopoly.

The antitrust laws do not work against big business. They allow great success and growth. They do not allow the limiting of competition. The laws do not allow monopolies. They make sure that small businesses have a chance to compete. They also protect the customer. The antitrust laws make sure that we have choices. They make sure that big businesses are not setting prices too high. They make sure we get the best goods and services for our money.

The Progressive Era lasted from about 1900 to 1920. World War I had begun in 1914. America entered the war in 1917. This brought an end to the Progressive movement. Americans focused on the war instead of changes at home.

The Progressive movement accomplished many things. It was able to improve the lives of workers, the poor, and the American public. It made positive changes in education and health care. Important changes were also made in government. Progressives changed government for the

Understanding Competition

There are four main types of business competition:

Monopoly: A business or group of businesses has the only supply of a good or service. The customer can buy only these goods or services.

Pure Competition: Many businesses make and sell similar goods and services. The customer has many choices about what to buy.

Monopolistic Competition: Competing businesses sell the same product or service. Each business has control over its type of good or service, but there are other choices.

Oligopoly: A small number of businesses control an industry. The automobile industry is an example of an oligopoly.

better. They worked hard to get into government positions. They made laws that helped the American public.

For several years after the war, government activity against trusts and big business was not very strong. Leaders could not agree on what to do about big business.

Shoppers at Macy's department store in New York City find thousands of goods to choose from in the store. By the 1920s, the defeat of most monopolies had made consumer goods more affordable. People had learned that they should make the government help all people in the country, not just big businesses.

Some leaders wanted to leave big business alone so that companies could prosper and grow. They believed that big business helped build a strong American nation. Others believed in the antitrust laws. They wanted control over big business. They believed this helped America because it kept competition going and prices down.

The Progressive movement, however, changed the American public. The public was now aware of unfair business practices such as trusts, monopolies, and mergers. The American public learned to make government work for it. The public pressured the government to bring big business under control. Cases continued to be brought against big business. The public made sure that government worked for the people and not just for big business.

Glossary

business (BIZ-nis) A company that makes or sells goods or services.

competition (kom-pih-TIH-shin) When two or more people or groups are trying to get the same thing.

competitor (kum-PEH-tih-ter) A group or person who is after the same thing as another group or person.

goods (GOODZ) Things that are made and sold.

merger (MUR-jur) The act of making two or more businesses into one.

monopoly (muh-NAH-puh-lee) The complete control of something, especially goods and services. The group or company that has such control is also a monopoly.

price-fixing (PRYS-fix-ing) When a group of businesses agree on the same price for a good or service for all customers.

progress (PRAH-gres) Forward movement; advancement.

service (SUR-vis) A system or way of providing something useful or needed.

settlement (SEH-tul-ment) An agreement or decision about something.

stock (STOK) A share of a company. The consumer invests in the company and receives a stock.

trust (TRUST) The combining of businesses or companies, especially to control and limit competition.

Web Sites

Due to the changing nature of Internet links, the Rosen Publishing Group, Inc., has developed an online list of Web sites related to the subject of this book. This site is updated regularly. Please use this link to access the list:

http://www.rosenlinks.com/pmnhnt/prtr

Primary Source Image List

Cover (top): Photograph of Theodore Roosevelt, circa 1906. Currently housed at the Library of Congress, Washington, D.C.

Cover (bottom): Photograph of the Standard Oil Company, Richmond, California, circa 1913. Currently housed at the Library of Congress, Washington, D.C.

Page 5 (left): Stereoscope of central New York, circa 1865. Currently housed at the New York Public Library.

Page 5 (right): Advertising pamphlet of the Anderson Shoe Factory, 1915.

Page 6: Photograph of logging camp in Stevens Pass, Washington, 1899.

Page 7: Photograph of John D. Rockefeller Sr., 1894.

Page 8: Cartoon illustration, "Who Is in the Soup Now?" by Dalrymple. In *Puck*, May 1, 1889.

Page 10: Illustration, "An Awful Battle at Homestead, Pa." In *National Police Gazette*, July 23, 1892. Currently housed at the Library of Congress, Washington, D.C.

Page 12: Cartoon illustration, "The Bosses of the Senate," by Joseph Keppler, January 23, 1889.

Page 15: Map of railroads in the United States, 1850. Currently housed at the New York Public Library.

Page 16: Cartoon illustration, "A Nauseating Job, But It Must Be Done," appearing in the *Saturday Globe* (Utica, New York), circa 1904.

Page 21 (left): Photograph, "Opening of the New York Stock Exchange," November 28, 1914.

Page 21 (inset): Photograph of meat inspectors at Swift & Company, Chicago, circa 1900.

Page 22: Photograph of front gate, Paramount Pictures, 1930. Private collection of Troy Taylor.

Index

About the Author

Bernadette Brexel is a freelance author living in New York City.